The COCKTAIL HOUR Coloring Book

by: Hannah Rothstein

ISBN 978-1-943649-00-6

For information about custom editions, special sales, and premium and corporate purchases, please contact Hannah Rothstein at art@hrothstein.com.

www.hrothstein.com

THE ART OF
Cocktails

An Out of the Box Introduction

No one likes a boring introduction. Actually, no one really likes an introduction, period. So, let's distill this to the essentials.

The book you now hold combines two wonderful ways to unwind — sipping cocktails and coloring. Serving up 16 classic cocktail recipes and 14 exclusive formulations from 6 artisanal beverage makers, this hands-on guide overflows with toast-worthy learnings and libations.

On each page of this elegant tome, you'll find a glass sectioned into patterns. Each pattern represents an ingredient, and its proportion within the glass indicates how much to add.

Capiche? Good. Pencils down, bottoms up, and enjoy!

THE CLASSICS

MOJITO

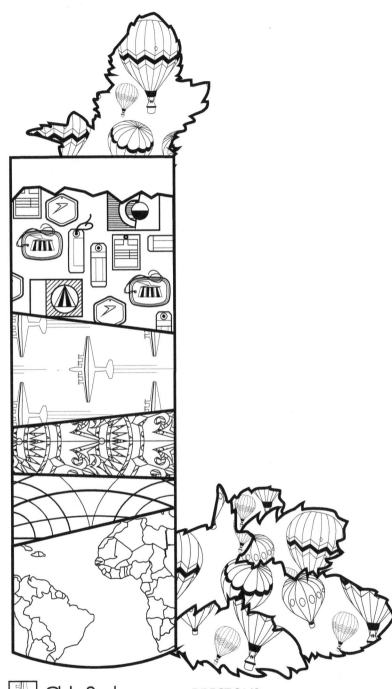

 White Rum

 Fresh Lime Juice

 Simple Syrup

 Club Soda

 Ice

 Fresh Mint

DIRECTIONS:
Muddle mint, lime, and simple syrup in cocktail shaker. Add rum and ice and shake vigorously. Top with club soda and garnish with mint.

JACK ROSE

 Apple Jack

 Fresh Lemon Juice

 Grenadine

Apple Slices

DIRECTIONS:
Pour liquids into cocktail shaker filled with ice. Shake. Strain into glass and garnish with apple slices.

MARTINI

 Gin or Vodka

 Dry Vermouth

 Olives

DIRECTIONS:
Pour liquids into a cocktail shaker filled with ice. Shake or stir. Strain into glass and garnish with olives.

GREYHOUND

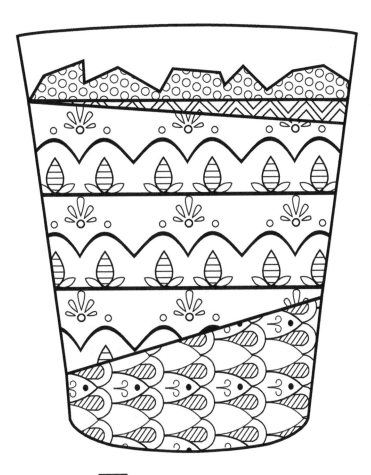

 Vodka

 Fresh Grapefruit Juice

 Simple Syrup (optional)

 Ice

DIRECTIONS:
Pour liquids into glass. Stir and top with ice.

DAIQUIRI

 White Rum

 Fresh Lime Juice

 Superfine Sugar

 Lime Wedge

DIRECTIONS:
Pour liquids into cocktail shaker. Add sugar and stir until dissolved. Top with ice and shake. Strain into chilled glass and garnish with lime wedge.

15

BLOODY MARY

DIRECTIONS:
Pour ingredients into cocktail shaker. Stir. Strain into glass filled with ice and garnish with celery and olives.

 Vodka

 Tomato Juice

 Fresh Lemon Juice

 Worcestershire Sauce

 Horseradish

 Salt & Pepper

 Ice

 Celery

 Olives

17

PORTO FLIP

 Brandy

 Red Port

 Egg Yolk

Nutmeg

DIRECTIONS:
Pour liquids and yolk into cocktail shaker filled with ice. Shake. Strain into glass and sprinkle with freshly grated nutmeg.

DARK AND STORMY

 Dark Rum

 Ginger Beer

 Ice

 Lime Wedges

DIRECTIONS:
Fill glass with ice. Pour in liquids.
Squeeze lime into glass and stir.

SIDECAR

 Cognac

 Triple Sec

 Fresh Lemon Juice

 Sugar

DIRECTIONS:
Pour liquids into cocktail shaker filled with ice. Shake. Strain into glass with sugar-coated rim.

CAIPIRINHA

 Lime Wedges

 Cachaça

 Superfine Sugar

 Ice

Lime Wheel

DIRECTIONS:
In glass, muddle lime wedges with sugar. Add cachaça and ice. Stir and garnish with lime wheel.

FRENCH 75

 Gin

 Fresh Lemon Juice

 Simple Syrup

 Brut Champange

DIRECTIONS:
Pour gin, lemon juice, and simple sryup into cocktail shaker filled with ice. Shake. Strain into glass and top with champagne..

MONKEY GLAND

 Gin

 Fresh OJ

 Grenadine

 Absinthe

Orange Slice

DIRECTIONS:
Pour liquids into cocktail shaker filled with ice. Shake. Strain into glass and garnish with orange slice.

SAZERAC

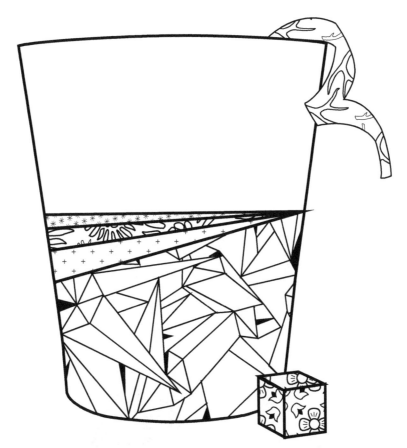

▢ Rye Whiskey

▢ Peychaud's Bitters

▢ Angostura Bitters

▢ Absinthe

▢ Sugar Cube

▢ Lemon Twist

DIRECTIONS:
In glass, muddle sugar with a few drops of water. Add ice cubes, rye whiskey, and bitters. Coat interoir of 2nd glass with absinthe. Strain into 2nd glass and garnish with lemon twist.

BLOODHOUND

 Gin

 Sweet Vermouth

 Dry Vermouth

 Crushed Strawberries

 Strawberries

DIRECTIONS:
Pour liquids and crushed strawberries into cocktail shaker filled with ice. Shake. Strain into glass and garnish with fresh strawberries.

PISCO SOUR

 Pisco

 Fresh Lemon Juice

Simple Syrup

Egg Whites

DIRECTIONS:
Pour ingredients into cocktail shaker filled with ice. Shake, and strain into glass. If desired, top with a few dashes of bitters.

IRISH COFFEE

 Hot Coffee

 Irish Whiskey

 Brown Sugar

 Whipped Cream

DIRECTIONS:
Pour coffee into glass or mug. Add sugar and stir until disolved. Mix in whiksey and top with whipped cream.

EXCLUSIVE RECIPES

SAN FRAN SODA

by Anchor Brewing & Distilling
& mixologist Devin Hardy of House of Blues Anaheim

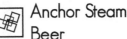 Hophead Vodka

Fresh Lime Juice

Soda Water

Anchor Steam Beer

Lemon Wedge

DIRECTIONS:
Fill pint glass with ice. Add vodka, lime, and soda water. Top with Anchor Steam Beer and garnish with lemon wedge.

CHERRY SHANDY

by Anchor Brewing & Distilling
& mixologist Emily Arden Wells of Gastronomista.com

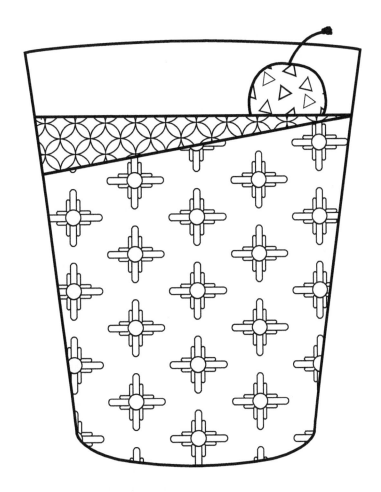

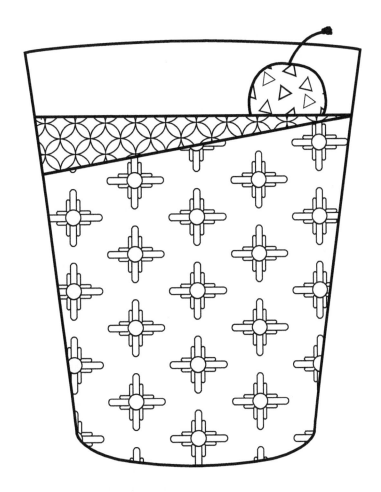 Anchor Brewing's Go West! IPA

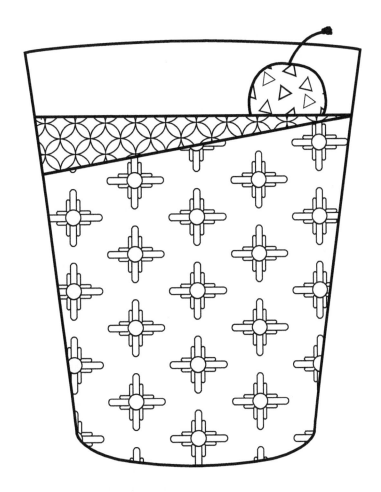 Luxardo Cherry Sangue Morlacco Liqueur

 Luxardo Cherry

DIRECTIONS:
Stir Go West! IPA and Luxardo Cherry Liquor in tumbler. Garnish with Luxardo cherry.

CALIFORNIA'S CALLIN'

by Anchor Brewing & Distilling & mixologist Jeff Hollinger

 Junipero Gin

 Grapefruit Juice

 Lemon Juice

 Luxardo Maraschino

 Tempus Fugit Abbott's Bitters

 Anchor California Lager

 Ice

 Grapefruit Peel

45

ROOT OF ALL EVIL

by St. George Spirits

 St. George
Absinthe Verte

Artisinal Root Beer

 Ice

Star Anise

DIRECTIONS:
Pour St. George Absinthe Verte into glass filled with ice. Top with root beer. Gradually let louche, or stir gently until consistently cloudy.

CAPTAIN AMERICANO

by St. George Spirits

 Bruto Americano

 Sweet Vermouth

 Soda Water

 Ice

 Orange Peel

DIRECTIONS:
Fill glass with ice. Add Bruto Americano and sweet vermouth, and top with soda. Stir gently and garnish with orange peel.

GREEN CHILE GIMLET

by St. George Spirits

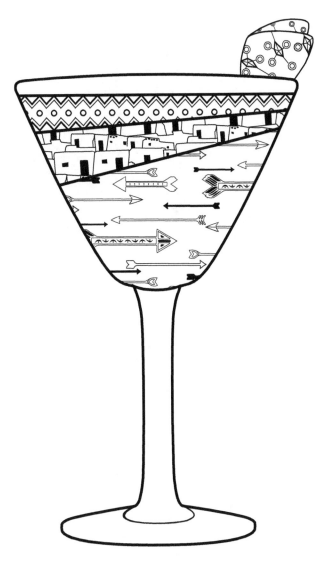

 St. George Green Chile Vodka

 Fresh Lime Juice

 Simple Syrup

 Lime Peel

DIRECTIONS:
Pour liquids into cocktail shaker filled with ice. Shake. Strain into chilled glass and garnish with lime peel.

MIAMI NICE

by DRY Sparkling

 Rum

 Cucumber DRY

 Ice

 Lime Wheel

 Mint

DIRECTIONS:
Muddle lime and mint in cocktail shaker. Add rum and ice. Shake. Pour into glass filled with ice and top with Cucumber DRY. Garnish with lime and mint.

THE STACI

by DRY Sparkling

 Bourbon

 Rainer Cherry DRY

 Ice

 Lemon Wedge

 Mint

DIRECTIONS:
Muddle lemon and mint in cocktail shaker. Add bourbon, shake, and pour into glass filled with ice. Top with Ranier Cherry DRY and garnish with mint.

THE L&L

DRY Sparkling

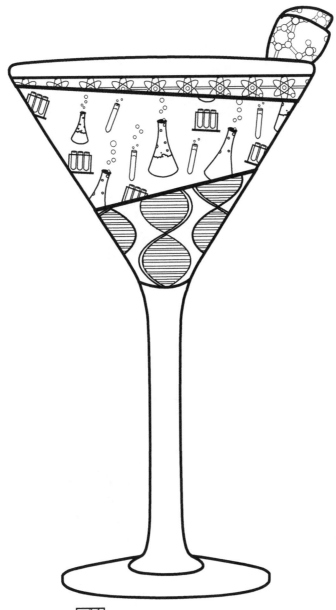

Vodka

 Lavender DRY

 St-Germain

 Lemon Peel

DIRECTIONS:
Pour vodka and St-Germain into cocktail shaker filled with ice. Shake, and strain into glass. Top with Lavendery DRY and garnish with lemon peel.

VANILLA MANHATTAN

by Middle West Spirits

 OYO Honey Vanilla Bean Vodka

 Navan Vanilla Liqueur

 Noilly Prat Sweet Vermouth

 Angostura Bitters

 Vanilla Bean

DIRECTIONS:
Pour liquids into cocktail shaker filled with ice. Stir. Strain into glass and garnish with vanilla bean..

WILD OYO

by Middle West Spirits

 OYO Bourbon

 Whiskey

 Simple Syrup

 Fresh Lime Juice

 Soda water

 Ice

 Lime Wheel

DIRECTIONS:
Pour OYO Bourbon, whiskey, simple syrup, and lime juice in large tumbler filled with ice. Top off with soda water and garnish with lime wheel.

PEARJUS

by Chandon

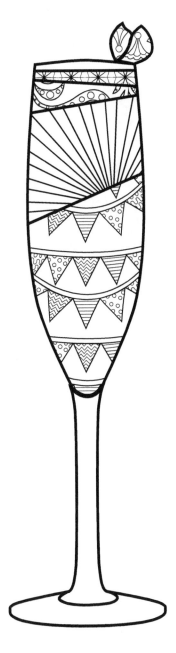

 Chandon Brut
Classic

 Pear Juice

 Maple Syrup

 Fresh Lemon
Juice

 Sage Leaves

DIRECTIONS:
Pour pear juice, 1/2 maple syrup, lemon juice, and 1 sage leaf into cocktail shaker filled with ice. Shake. Strain into glass and add remaining maple syrup.. Top with Chandon Brut Classic and garnish with sage leaf.

PRICKLY PEAR

by Chandon

 Chadon Rosé

 Lemonade

 Prickly Pear Juice

 Agave Syrup

 Lemon Twist

DIRECTIONS:
Pour agave syrup, prickly pear juice and lemon juice into cocktail shaker filled with ice. Shake, and strain into glass. Top with Chandon Rosé and garnish with lemon twist.

HANKY PANKY

by Fernet Branca

 Fernet-Branca

 Antica Formula Vermouth

Sipsmith Gin

  Orange Twist

DIRECTIONS:
Pour gin, vermouth, and Fernet-Branca into mixing glass filled with ice. Stir. Strain into chilled glass and garnish with orange twist.

ABOUT THE AUTHOR

Known for her internet art including Thanksgiving Special, Broga, and Dr. Dreidel, Hannah Rothstein is a conceptual artist and painter. Her pieces have been featured in TIME, The Guardian, The Huffington Post, Fast Company, Slate, This Is Colossal, and more.

Hannah's first book, "Yoga for Bros," was released by Sterling Publishing in June 2016.

Currently living in Berkeley, CA, Hannah spends a lot time of biking, climbing, wearing costumes, talking to strangers and delivering ridiculous karaoke performances.

See more of Hannah's work on Instagram @hrothsteinart or at www.hrothstein.com.

BRAND PARTNERS

Anchor Brewing & Distilling
San Francisco, CA
www.anchorbrewing.com
www.anchordistilling.com

St. George Spirits
Alameda, CA
www.stgeorgespirits.com

DRY Sparkling
Seattle, WA
www.drysparkling.com

Chandon
Yountville, CA
www.chandon.com

Middle West Spirits
Colombus, OH
www. middlewestspirits.com

Fernet-Branca
Milan, Italy
www.branca.it

CPSIA information can be obtained
at www.ICGtesting.com
Printed in the USA
LVHW062205261119
638663LV00017B/1012/P